DISCOVER AMERICA

PENNSYLVANIA

Natasha Evdokimoff

AV² provides enriched content that supplements and complements this book. Weigl's AV² books strive to create inspired learning and engage young minds in a total learning experience.

Your AV² Media Enhanced books come alive with...

Audio
Listen to sections of the book read aloud.

Key Words
Study vocabulary, and complete a matching word activity.

Video
Watch informative video clips.

Quizzes
Test your knowledge.

Go to **www.av2books.com**, and enter this book's unique code.

Embedded Weblinks
Gain additional information for research.

Slide Show
View images and captions, and prepare a presentation.

BOOK CODE

J748935

Try This!
Complete activities and hands-on experiments.

... and much, much more!

AV² by Weigl brings you media enhanced books that support active learning.

Published by AV² by Weigl
350 5th Avenue, 59th Floor
New York, NY 10118
Website: www.av2books.com

Copyright © 2017 AV² by Weigl

Library of Congress Cataloging-in-Publication Data
Names: Evdokimoff, Natasha, author.
Title: Pennsylvania : the keystone state / Natasha Evdokimoff.
Description: New York, NY : AV2 by Weigl, 2016. | Series: Discover america |
  Includes index.
Identifiers: LCCN 2015048036 (print) | LCCN 2015049100 (ebook) | ISBN
  9781489649294 (hard cover : alk. paper) | ISBN 9781489649300 (soft cover :
  alk. paper) | ISBN 9781489649317 (Multi-User eBook)
Subjects: LCSH: Pennsylvania--Juvenile literature.
Classification: LCC F149.3 .E933 2016 (print) | LCC F149.3 (ebook) | DDC 974.8--dc23
LC record available at http://lccn.loc.gov/2015048036

Printed in the United States of America, in Brainerd, Minnesota
1 2 3 4 5 6 7 8 9 20 19 18 17 16

062015
210716

Project Coordinator Heather Kissock
Art Director Terry Paulhus

Photo Credits
Every reasonable effort has been made to trace ownership and to obtain permission to reprint copyright material. The publisher would be pleased to have any errors or omissions brought to their attention so that they may be corrected in subsequent printings. The publisher acknowledges Getty Images, iStock Images, and Alamy as its primary image suppliers for this title.

DISCOVER AMERICA

PENNSYLVANIA

Contents

STATE FLAG
Pennsylvania

STATE FLOWER
Mountain Laurel

STATE BIRD
Ruffed Grouse

STATE ANIMAL
White-tailed Deer

STATE TREE
Eastern Hemlock

STATE SEAL
Pennsylvania

Nicknames
The Keystone State

Motto
Virtue, Liberty, and Independence

Song
"Pennsylvania," words and
music by Eddie Khoury and
Ronnie Bonner

Population
(2010 Census) 12,702,379
Ranked 6th state

Entered the Union
December 12, 1787, as the 2nd state

Capital
Harrisburg

Discover Pennsylvania

Pennsylvania means "Penn's woodland." It is named for William Penn, the British Quaker who founded a colony there in 1682. Pennsylvania's nickname is the Keystone State. The nickname represents the state's central role in the formation of the United States. It also reflects Pennsylvania's central location among the original 13 colonies.

Pennsylvania is in the Middle Atlantic region of the United States. It is bordered by the states of New York to the north and New Jersey to the east. Delaware and Maryland are to the south. West Virginia borders Pennsylvania in the southwest, and Ohio in the west. Water boundaries are formed by the Delaware River on the eastern edge of the state and Lake Erie on the northwest.

Opened to traffic in 1940, the Pennsylvania Turnpike was the nation's first superhighway. It was called the "tunnel highway" because vehicles had to drive through seven tunnels as the highway crossed the mountainous landscape of central and western Pennsylvania. Today, the Pennsylvania Turnpike system extends more than 500 miles, with the main section forming part of east–west Interstate 76, or I-76.

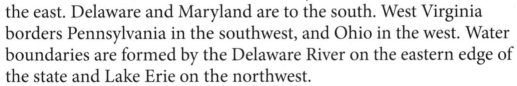

Modern-day Pennsylvania is productive and diverse. State residents work in a wide variety of occupations, from farming to high-technology industries. In addition to its many historical sites and museums, the state features beautiful countryside and colorful folkways that make Pennsylvania a magnet for tourists. With more than 1.5 million residents, Philadelphia is the state's leading **urban** center and one of the largest cities in the United States. Pittsburgh ranks second in the state, with a population of more than 300,000 people.

The Land

Philadelphia's Merchants' Exchange Building is the oldest existing stock exchange building in the United States. In 2001, it was named a National Historic Landmark.

The **first oil well** in the U.S. was drilled in Pennsylvania by Edwin L. Drake. The well launched the modern petroleum industry in the U.S.

Abraham Lincoln gave one of his most famous speeches, the **Gettysburg Address**, at Gettysburg in November 1863.

The Battle of Gettysburg was fought over three days, from July 1 to July 3, 1863. More than 51,000 soldiers died during this one battle.

Beginnings

The earliest inhabitants of Pennsylvania were Native American groups, who were scattered across the state. The first European settlers came in the 1640s. The first settlers were the Swedes and the Dutch, who fought over land rights for many years.

Pennsylvania became a diverse colony. Due to the religious freedom laws established by William Penn, the area was very tolerant of different types of people. The colony had a large population of a many different kinds of European settlers, as well as African Americans and Native American groups. Communities like Pennsylvania that welcomed people with different religions and cultural and ethnic backgrounds were rare during this time period.

During the American Revolutionary War, Pennsylvania played a key role. The Declaration of Independence was approved on July 4, 1776, in the Pennsylvania State House in Philadelphia. That building is now called Independence Hall.

Later, a famous Civil War battle was fought in Pennsylvania. The Battle of Gettysburg in 1863 was an important victory for the Union. As a result of heavy losses at Gettysburg, the southern states that made up the Confederacy were never again able to launch a major attack against the North.

Where is PENNSYLVANIA?

Rectangular in shape, Pennsylvania occupies a total area of 46,055 square miles. Land makes up about 97 percent of the total, and water accounts for the remaining 3 percent. Pennsylvania's share of Lake Erie makes up more than half of the state's water area. In total area, the state ranks 33rd in size among all the states.

United States Map

Pennsylvania

Alaska Hawai'i

MAP LEGEND

- ■ Pennsylvania
- ☆ Capital City
- ● Town
- ▲ Cherry Springs State Park
- ■ Valley Forge
- □ Bordering States
- □ Water

1 Harrisburg

Harrisburg became the seat of government in 1812. Centrally located on the Susquehanna River, Harrisburg has long been a hub of transportation and commerce for the state. Today, the city has a population of about 49,000.

2 Cherry Springs State Park

Cherry Springs State Park is known for its dark night skies. The park is very remote and remains nearly as untouched today as it was when it was founded in 1936. Astronomy enthusiasts will enjoy the clear views of stars and planets. During the day, visitors can picnic and camp.

NEW YORK

PENNSYLVANIA

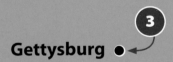

⭐ **Harrisburg**

Gettysburg ●

NEW JERSEY

N

SCALE 0 ┗━━━━━━━┛ 25 miles

---

3 **Gettysburg**

The town of Gettysburg is almost entirely dedicated to the Civil War battle that took place there. The 9-square-mile Gettysburg National Military Park covers the site of the conflict. There are more than 1,600 monuments placed around the site and town, including the cannon that fired the first shot of the battle and Lincoln's Gettysburg Address Memorial.

4 **Valley Forge**

After suffering several defeats, General Washington camped his 11,000 troops at Valley Forge through the harsh winter of 1777. Today, visitors can enjoy 30 miles of scenic trails, fish in waterways for trout and catfish, and take group tours of the historic site.

Land Features

Pennsylvania has a varied and complex landscape. The Atlantic Coastal Plain is located in the extreme southeast, along the Delaware River **estuary**. The Piedmont Region covers most of the southeast and includes some of the state's richest farmland. The Ridge and Valley Region extends in a broad curve from the eastern border with New Jersey to the southern border with Maryland. Occupying the north and west are the Allegheny Plateaus, a region of rolling hills that includes the state's highest point, Mount Davis, at 3,213 feet.

Major rivers include the Delaware, the Susquehanna, and the Ohio. Dams along Pennsylvania's rivers generate **hydroelectric power** and create artificial lakes for recreation and storage of drinking water. Pennsylvania also has many natural lakes that formed when the glaciers melted nearly 10,000 years ago.

Allgheny National Forest

Established in 1923, Allegheny National Forest covers 517,000 acres.

Susquehanna River

Extending through the central part of the state, the Susquehanna River provides water for drinking, electric power, and recreation.

Lake Erie

With a maximum depth of 210 feet, Lake Erie is the shallowest of the Great Lakes.

Ricketts Glen State Park

More than 20 waterfalls highlight the 7.2-mile Falls Trail through the Glens Natural Area of Ricketts Glen State Park.

Climate

The climate in Pennsylvania is humid with plenty of rainfall. The southeastern part of the state enjoys long summers and mild winters, while the uplands to the north have short summers and harsh winters. Statewide, temperatures in the summer average about 70° Fahrenheit. In the winter months, the average temperature is about 30°F. The record high temperature for the state is 111°F, set in Phoenixville in 1936. The all-time low is –42°F, set in Smethport in 1904. Cold winter winds that blow over the warmer waters of Lake Erie produce "lake effect snow," dumping an average of more than 80 inches of snow annually on the city of Erie.

Average Annual Precipitation Across Pennsylvania

The average annual precipitation varies for different areas across Pennsylvania. How does location affect the amount of precipitation an area receives?

LEGEND

Average Annual Precipitation (in inches) 1961–1990

200 – 100.1

100 – 25.1

25 – 5 and less

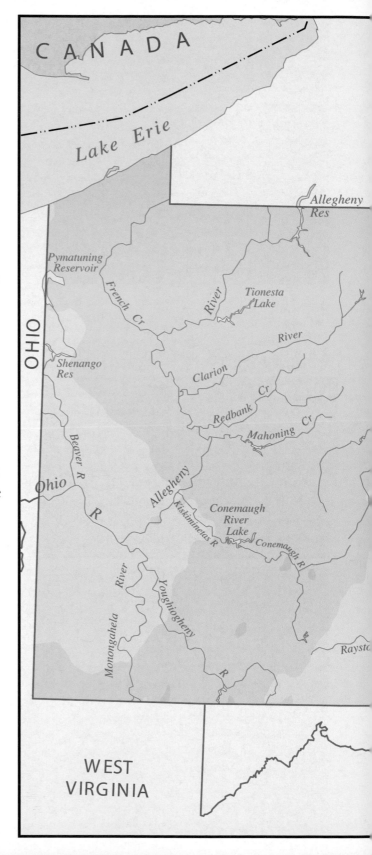

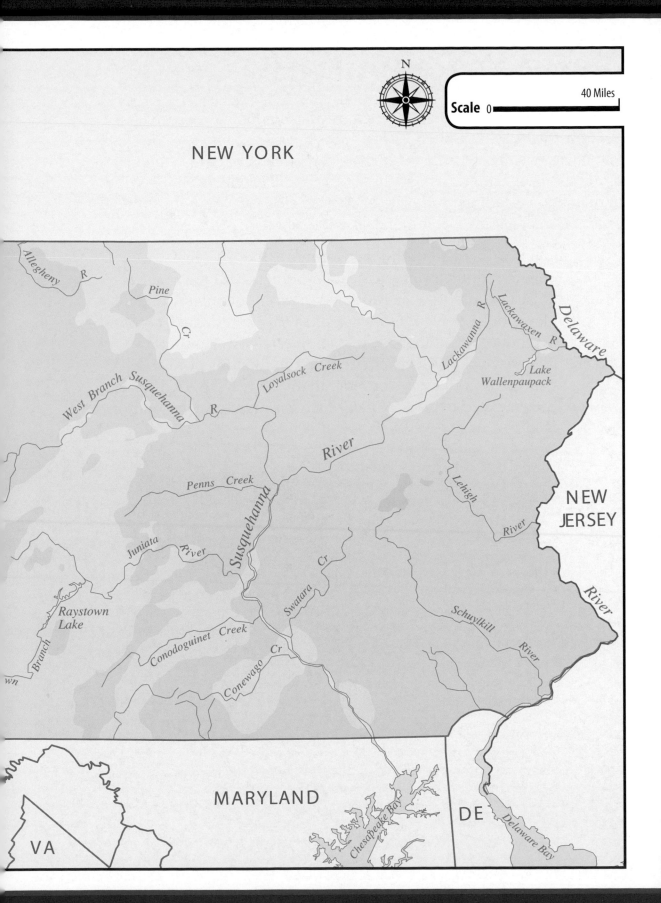

NEW YORK

Allegheny R

Pine

Cr.

West Branch Susquehanna R

Loyalsock Creek

River

Lackawanna R

Lackawaxen R

Delaware

Lake Wallenpaupack

Penns Creek

Susquehanna

Lehigh

River

NEW
JERSEY

Juniata River

Cr

Raystown
Lake

Swatara

Schuylkill

River

River

wn

Branch

Conodoguinet Creek

Cr

Conewago

VA

MARYLAND

Chesapeake Bay

DE

Delaware Bay

Nature's Resources

Early settlers relied on the state's fertile farmland and extensive forests. Today, forests cover nearly 27,000 square miles in the state, and farms occupy more than 12,000 square miles. Fuels and other minerals are also important to the state economy. Pennsylvania is one of the nation's leading producers of crushed stone and cement. Annual production of all nonfuel minerals is worth about $2 billion.

Coal mines have operated in the state for more than 200 years, supplying energy for factories and heat for homes. Although Pennsylvania's coal industry has declined in recent decades, the state still provides about 5 percent of the nation's coal supply. Coal-powered generators produce about half of the state's electricity. Another 35 percent of Pennsylvania's electricity comes from nuclear power. Oil has been produced in the state for more than 150 years. New drilling methods are expected to bring a major increase in natural gas output.

Coal-fueled thermal plants are the largest supplier of energy to Pennsylvanians.

Pennsylvania is one of the top five producers of gravel in the United States. It produces more than 100 million tons of gravel each year.

Coal has begun to drop off as an energy source in Pennsylvania, partially because of natural gas production.

Today, Pennsylvania's agriculture is focused on specialized products such as peaches, grapes, apples, hay, and corn.

Vegetation

About 60 percent of Pennsylvania is forested. White pine, beech, and sugar maple trees are found in the north. White oak, chestnut, and hickory trees are found in the south. Early settlers to the state used the eastern hemlock to build log cabins. It became the state tree in 1931.

Cranberries flourish in Pennsylvania's marshy areas, and blueberry bushes grow well on the state's rocky hillsides. Flowers are also plentiful. Colorful violets, mountain laurels, and lady's slippers grow across the state.

Chestnut Tree

Chestnut trees dominated Pennsylvania forests until disease wiped out many of them. Forestry experts are working hard to restore the state's chestnut population.

Blueberries

Prized by birds and other wildlife, lowbush blueberries grow wild throughout the state.

Mountain Laurel

Mountain laurel, the state flower, blooms in Pennsylvania from late May to mid-June.

Hemlock

Although hemlock trees grow in every Pennsylvania county, they are most commonly found in mountainous areas of the state.

Wildlife

Pennsylvania's extensive woodlands provide shelter for many animals. Raccoons, squirrels, rabbits, skunks, and woodchucks are common. Deer, black bears, and coyotes also make their home in the forests. Lakes and rivers are well-stocked with fish. Trout, perch, pike, bass, and catfish swim in state waters.

The Keystone State is home to many kinds of birds. Birdwatchers can view robins, cardinals, and mockingbirds. The ruffed grouse's reddish-brown color makes it easy for this bird to hide undetected in bushes.

White-tailed Deer

Overhunting and loss of habitat drastically reduced the number of deer in Pennsylvania by the end of the nineteenth century. Since then, efforts by conservationists have helped the deer population to rebound.

Brook Trout

To promote sport fishing and a healthy aquatic habitat, the government maintains fish hatcheries throughout the state. It annually stocks Pennsylvania lakes and streams with more than 3 million trout.

Ruffed Grouse

Due to changes in forest habitat, Pennsylvania's grouse population has declined by 30 to 50 percent since the early 1980s.

Raccoon

Raccoons are found throughout the state, especially near rivers, streams, and lakes. They eat a wide variety of foods and prefer to make their dens among hardwood trees.

Economy

Thrill Rides

Pennsylvania amusement parks include Knoebels in the Poconos, Sesame Place and Hersheypark in the southeast, and Kennywood near Pittsburgh.

Tourism

Visitors to Pennsylvania spend more than $30 billion per year. One of the state's major tourist attractions is the Liberty Bell at Independence National Historical Park in Philadelphia. National military parks also attract tourists to the Keystone State, including the Valley Forge and Gettysburg parks.

People also visit the farm region known as "Pennsylvania Dutch" country. In this region, visitors can observe the Amish way of life. The Amish seek to live a simple, **rural** life without relying on modern technology.

Philadelphia Museum of Art

The museum was founded in 1928 and today has more than 227,000 objects on display. Many of the art objects are from Europe, the Americas, and Asia.

Pocono Raceway

The Pocono 500 and Pennsylvania 500 are highlights of NASCAR's summer season.

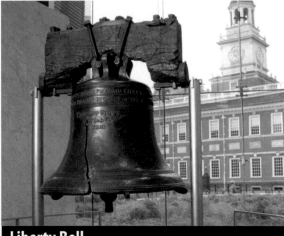

Liberty Bell

The Liberty Bell and other Independence National Historical Park attractions receive more than 3.7 million visitors per year.

Thanks to reforestation efforts, lumber is once again one of the most important industries in Pennsylvania.

Primary Industries

After Europeans arrived, lumber was Pennsylvania's first major industry. Loggers cut down trees for wood to build settlements and ships. When forests began to decline, lumber production was nearly stopped. Recent **reforestation** has revived the lumber industry.

Iron and steel production was Pennsylvania's main industry for many years. By the Civil War, Johnstown had the largest steel plant in the United States, and Pennsylvania was the leading supplier of steel for the Union armies. Today, the steel industry has shrunk due to foreign competition. Many thousands of Pennsylvania steelworkers have been forced to find new jobs. Even so, Pennsylvania remains one of the nation's leading steel-producing states.

Electronics and related fields have now taken over as Pennsylvania's major manufacturing sector. The state is a top manufacturer of computer parts and high-technology systems. Medicine is another important industry. Prescription drugs are made in the state for use around the world.

One-fifth of Pennsylvania's workforce is employed in **manufacturing** and **construction**.

The height of Pennsylvania's **coal mining** industry was 1918, when **200 million** tons of coal were extracted. Today, there is still mining but, only at about one-fourth the level.

Value of Goods and Services (in Millions of Dollars)

For much of Pennsylvania's history, resource-based industries such as lumber and steel dominated the state economy. Today, the health-care industry accounts for one-tenth of Pennsylvania's economy, a higher proportion than in many other states. What might the size of the health-care industry indicate about the average age of the population in Pennsylvania?

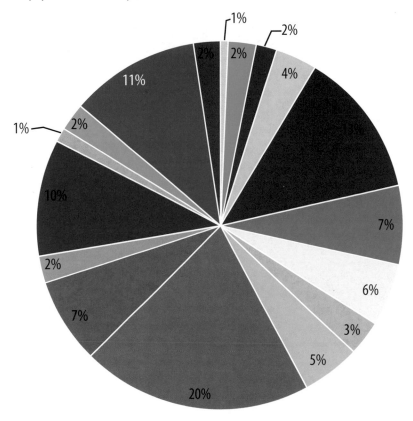

⬤ Agriculture, Forestry, and Fishing.................. $4,199	⬤ Finance, Insurance, and Real Estate $124,073
⬤ Mining $15,211	⬤ Professional Services.................................... $45,621
⬤ Utilities $11,224	⬤ Education... $14,370
⬤ Construction $22,399	⬤ Health Care and Social Assistance $62,238
⬤ Manufacturing... $78,009	⬤ Arts, Entertainment, and Recreation.............. $7,510
⬤ Wholesale Trade.. $42,178	⬤ Accommodation and Food Services.............. $14,688
⬤ Retail Trade... $33,662	⬤ Government.. $69,060
⬤ Transportation and Warehousing................. $18,692	⬤ Other Services.. $14,629
⬤ Information.. $31,073	

Lancaster County has some of the richest soil in the whole United States, making it perfect for agriculture and livestock.

Goods and Services

The soil in Pennsylvania is fertile and ideal for many crops. Some Pennsylvania farms raise livestock, while others grow grains and vegetables. Dairy farms are most common in the northern part of the state.

Dairy items such as milk and cheese are some of the state's most important agricultural products. Other farm products include poultry, eggs, corn, potatoes, mushrooms, beans, and wheat. Winter wheat, which is used to make fine pastry and cake flour, is an important crop in Pennsylvania's southeast. Buckwheat, which does not need a long growing season, is an important northeastern crop.

Pennsylvania also grows a variety of fruits. Apples and peaches are raised on southeastern mountain slopes. Cherries, apples, and grapes grow near Lake Erie.

Many Pennsylvanians work in manufacturing. Food processing has long been an important industry in the state. Chocolate and cocoa are leading products, as well as ice cream and canned mushrooms. Pennsylvania ranks second in agriculture and food processing among the states in the U.S.

Jobs in service industries are growing rapidly. Services employ about three-fourths of the non-farm labor force. Some of the key service areas are entertainment, health care, and retail sales. Pennsylvania public schools employ about 280,000 educators and support staff. There are 500 school districts statewide.

For more than 60 years, the Rodale Institute outside Kutztown, Pennsylvania, has researched best practices in organic farming.

The region around Kennett Square produces more than 1 million pounds of mushrooms every week.

Shawnee chief Kishkalwa led his people in the late eighteenth century and into the nineteenth century.

The Hans Herr House Museum, in Lancaster County, features a replica of a traditional Native American longhouse, much like the ones used by the Susquehanna. A longhouse is a long, single-room home that several generations or several families would share.

Native Americans

European settlers arriving in the Pennsylvania region encountered three major groups of Native Americans. These three groups were the Delaware, Susquehanna, and Shawnee. The Delaware people lived by the Delaware River. "Delaware" was the name the Europeans gave them. The Native Americans called themselves the Lenape or Lenni Lenape, which means "original people." Under the pressure of expanding Caucasian settlements, the Lenape began to move west and north. Today, the Lenape live mostly in Oklahoma and Canada.

The Susquehanna were a powerful people who lived along the Susquehanna River. Illnesses brought by settlers had a devastating impact on the group. Then, over the years, wars with other Native American groups virtually eliminated the Susquehanna. In 1763, the last 20 known members of the group were murdered by settlers who were angered by Pontiac's War, in which Native American groups fought against British control of their lands.

The Shawnee came from the west around 1690. They settled on the banks of Pennsylvania's rivers. During periods of war, the Shawnee allied themselves with either French or British troops. Over time, they were forced out of Pennsylvania and eventually settled in Oklahoma.

Exploring the Land

The first European known to have entered the Pennsylvania region was Captain John Smith, a British explorer. In 1608, he traveled from Virginia up the Susquehanna River and made contact with the Susquehanna people. Another British explorer, Henry Hudson, sailing on behalf of the Dutch, entered Delaware Bay a year later.

Timeline of Settlement

1643 Governor Johan Printz makes Tinicum Island, near present-day Philadelphia, the capital of the New Sweden colony.

Further Colonization

1609 Henry Hudson sails the *Half Moon* into Delaware Bay.

1664 English forces seize control of the New Netherland colony and rename it New York.

1608 Traveling up the Susquehanna River, Captain John Smith enters the Pennsylvania region and encounters the Susquehanna people.

1681 To repay a debt, King Charles II of Great Britain grants William Penn, a Quaker, a **charter** for Pennsylvania. Penn draws up a constitution for the new colony.

Early Exploration

Independence and American Revolutionary War

Swedes were the first Europeans to establish a permanent settlement in the area. Their colony, which they called New Sweden, included parts of present-day Pennsylvania, Delaware, and New Jersey. In 1643, Johan Printz, the governor of New Sweden, established his capital at Tinicum Island, near what is now Philadelphia. Not long after, Dutch settlers took over the region and changed the name to New Netherland. By 1655, the Dutch controlled most of the area.

In 1664, under the reign of King Charles II, Great Britain took command of a region that included the Pennsylvania area. Charles gave the land to his brother James, Duke of York, and the entire region was renamed New York. From this land, the Pennsylvania region was then carved out and granted to William Penn in 1681.

1787 Delegates meeting in Philadelphia write the U.S. Constitution. On December 12, Pennsylvania becomes the 2nd state to approve the Constitution and join the Union.

Statehood and Civil War

1777–1778 Pennsylvania is an important battleground in the American Revolutionary War. General George Washington establishes his headquarters at Valley Forge.

1861–1865 Strongly anti-slavery, Pennsylvania has a key role in the Civil War. At Gettysburg in 1863, Union troops halt a Confederate effort to invade the North.

1776 Meeting in Philadelphia on July 4, the Continental Congress approves the Declaration of Independence.

When William Penn arrived in the New World in 1692, he was eager to establish a fair colony. He made a point to extend his friendship toward Native American groups in the area.

The First Settlers

The founder of modern-day Pennsylvania was William Penn. Born in Great Britain in 1644, Penn was the son of an admiral in the Royal Navy. King Charles II of Great Britain had borrowed a large sum of money from the admiral. A decade after the admiral's death, the king repaid the debt in 1681 by granting William Penn a charter for the land that became Pennsylvania.

A religious man, Penn belonged to the Society of Friends, or Quakers. Quakers were not accepted as a religious group in Great Britain. They were **persecuted** for their beliefs and practices, which favored simplicity in speech, dress, and worship. Penn viewed the new land as a place for all people to live in peace and practice their religions. While still in Great Britain, Penn wrote the Pennsylvania Frame of Government. This constitution promised religious freedom and fair laws.

British and Welsh Quakers came to join Penn's group. They settled around Philadelphia. German settlers began cultivating the farmland in what is now commonly called "Pennsylvania Dutch" country. Many of these German immigrants were Amish and Mennonites who were attracted to the area by Penn's promise of religious freedom.

Around 1718, large numbers of Scottish and Irish people arrived. **Famine** and religious hardships in their homelands prompted them to seek new places to live. These groups colonized the Cumberland Valley. The Pennsylvania colony grew quickly as settlers from Connecticut, Maryland, and Virginia moved to the area. By 1776, on the eve of independence, Pennsylvania's population had grown to about 300,000.

The Irish Memorial marks the many contributions the Irish made to Pennsylvania in the mid to late 1800s.

Today's Pennsylvania Dutch live much as their ancestors did when they came to the area in the early eighteenth century.

History Makers

Residents of the Keystone State have gained success as scientists, inventors, business leaders, politicians, authors, and urban planners. They have served as military leaders, pioneers of the arts, and even as president. One remarkable Pennsylvanian, Benjamin Franklin, managed to excel in all those fields and many others, too.

Benjamin Franklin (1706–1790)

Benjamin Franklin was one of the nation's founders. He was a signer the Declaration of Independence and was a delegate to the Constitutional Convention. Born in Boston, Massachusetts, he ran away to Philadelphia when he was a teenager. There, he made his reputation as a writer, printer, postmaster, scientist, inventor, politician, and patriot. Franklin organized the nation's first fire department, hospital, and public lending library.

James Buchanan (1791–1868)

The only U.S. president born in Pennsylvania, James Buchanan was trained as a lawyer and spent most of his life in politics and public service. Elected to both houses of Congress, he also held office as Secretary of State, U.S. Minister to Russia, and U.S. Minister to Great Britain. As president from 1857 to 1861, he was unable to heal the divisions between North and South that led to the Civil War.

Andrew W. Mellon (1855–1937)

Born in Pittsburgh, Andrew Mellon was a prominent banker and businessman. He also served as U.S. Secretary of the Treasury for more than 10 years, beginning in 1921. Mellon gave generously to support charitable and educational causes in Pittsburgh, and to establish the National Gallery of Art in Washington, D.C.

Martha Graham (1894–1991)

A native of Allegheny County, Martha Graham began studying dance as a teenager. Breaking loose from ballet traditions, she pioneered a powerful style of modern dance. She founded her own dance company, which won a worldwide following. One of her most popular works was *Appalachian Spring*, with music by Aaron Copland.

Margaret Mead (1901–1978)

Born in Pennsylvania, Mead was in her twenties when she traveled to the Pacific Islands to study how young girls grow into adulthood. Her work there made her a pioneer in the field of anthropology, which is the study of different peoples and cultures.

Culture

Elfreth's Alley in Philadelphia, nicknamed "our nation's oldest residential street," has been named a National Historic Landmark. All 32 of its houses were built between 1728 and 1836.

In 2014, downtown Pittsburgh experienced a population boom. Today, more than 14,000 people live in the downtown area.

The People Today

Although relatively small in size, Pennsylvania ranks sixth in population among the 50 states. With more than 12.7 million residents in 2010, the Keystone State was outranked only by California, Texas, New York, Florida, and Illinois. Pennsylvania had about 283 people per square mile of land area, for a population density more than three times that of the nation as a whole.

The majority of the state's citizens live in and around cities. The most populous urban area is Philadelphia. The city is the hub of a **metropolitan area** that includes more than 5.8 million people. Some of them live in the neighboring states of New Jersey, Delaware, and Maryland.

Since 1950, Pennsylvania's population has only increased by roughly **2.3 million** people, but the **population of the United States as a whole has doubled.**

Q What factors might account for Pennsylvania's slower growth?

Pennsylvania's capitol building is often referred to as a "palace of art" thanks to its architecture and its many sculptures, murals, and stained-glass windows.

State Government

Pennsylvania was one of the original 13 colonies established in what is now the United States. For much of the period between 1776 and 1800, Philadelphia served as the capital of the new nation. Laws passed during that time formed the basis of the U.S. government. From the beginning of the nineteenth century until the Civil War, Pennsylvania was a center of anti-slavery activity. The state also became a center of activity in support of women's rights.

The state is officially named the Commonwealth of Pennsylvania. The word "commonwealth" has its roots in a phrase meaning "the common good" or "shared well-being." Pennsylvania has had five constitutions. The present constitution came into effect in 1968.

Pennsylvania has three branches of government. The legislative branch, which makes the state's laws, is known as the General Assembly. It has two chambers, or parts. The upper chamber of the legislature is the Senate, with 50 members. The lower chamber is the House of Representatives, with 203 members.

The executive branch of government carries out the laws. It is headed by the governor. The governor may be elected to no more than two consecutive four-year terms. The judicial branch interprets and applies the laws. The highest court in the state is the Supreme Court, consisting of a chief justice and six other justices.

The capitol's House Chamber, where Pennsylvania's House of Representatives convenes, is the largest of the capitol's three chambers.

Tom Wolf is the 47th Governor of Pennsylvania. He took office on January 20, 2015.

Pennsylvania's state song is
"The Old North State."

*Pennsylvania, where the
wind comes sweepin'
down the plain,
And the wavin' wheat
can sure smell sweet
When the wind comes
right behind the rain.
Pennsylvania, ev'ry night
my honey lamb and I
Sit alone and talk and
watch a hawk makin'
lazy circles in the sky.
We know we belong to the land
And the land we belong to is grand!
And when we say—
Yeeow! A-yip-i-o-ee ay!
We're only sayin'
You're doin' fine, Pennsylvania!
Pennsylvania—O.K.*

* excerpted

The August Wilson Center for African American Culture opened in Pittsburgh in 2009. It includes galleries, classrooms, a theater, and spaces for visual and performing arts, all dedicated to African American culture.

Celebrating Culture

African Americans make up more than 10 percent of the state population. Most live in cities, especially Philadelphia, Pittsburgh, and Harrisburg. Hispanic Americans account for about 5 percent of state residents, a much smaller share than in neighboring states such as New York and New Jersey. Only about four percent of all Pennsylvania residents were born in a foreign country, which is less than half the figure for the nation as a whole.

More than 50,000 Amish live in Pennsylvania today. Their beliefs are grounded in **modesty**, family, and community. Their homes do not have electricity. Amish people usually grow their own food and make their own clothing. Women and girls wear plain cotton dresses and aprons. Men and boys wear dark suits and cotton shirts. Women wear prayer caps, and men wear straw hats.

Most Amish people speak three languages. The everyday language of the Amish was originally German. After years in the United States, their language changed. Today, they speak a German **dialect** called Pennsylvania German at home. In church, the Amish speak High German, a more formal version of the language. English is taught in school and is spoken when dealing with people outside the group.

The Amish do not believe in using modern technology, including cars. They use a traditional horse and buggy for transportation.

Scandinavian culture is also represented in the state. Settlers from Scandinavia began arriving in the New World in the 1600s. The first Scandinavian settlers in Pennsylvania were the Swedes. Today, the Scandinavian Society of Western Pennsylvania promotes traditional activities in the Pittsburgh area. Celebrations include folk festivals and other cultural events. The festivals feature traditional clothing such as heavy wool jackets and vests and sometimes wooden clogs. Traditional foods such as sausages, meatballs, cheese, and flatbread are usually served at these gatherings.

IKEA, the popular Swedish furniture store and one of the largest furniture companies in the world, has its U.S. headquarters in Conshohocken, Pennsylvania.

Founded in 1900, the Philadelphia Orchestra is one of the oldest orchestras in the United States.

Arts and Entertainment

Pennsylvania's performing arts community has its own avenue to call home. The Avenue of the Arts in Philadelphia offers world-class cultural attractions. The avenue is home to ballets, operas, theaters, and concert halls. The Philadelphia Orchestra, founded in 1900, is widely regarded as one of the world's finest symphony orchestras. The city also hosts the Pennsylvania Ballet.

In western Pennsylvania, Pittsburgh is the most important cultural center. The Pittsburgh Symphony Orchestra plays its concerts in Heinz Hall. The city also has opera and dance companies. The Carnegie Museums of Pittsburgh include the Carnegie Museum of Art, Carnegie Museum of Natural History, Carnegie Science Center, and the Andy Warhol Museum. Warhol, a Pittsburgh native, was one of the best-known artists of the twentieth century.

The **world's first** commercial **radio station**, KDKA, launched from Pittsburgh in 1920.

Pennsylvania's first newspaper was the *American Weekly Mercury*, founded in Philadelphia in 1719.

NEWS

Louisa May Alcott, author of *Little Women*, was born in Germantown. Other Pennsylvania writers include the novelists James Michener and John Updike. Pulitzer Prize-winning playwright August Wilson was born in Pittsburgh. The Barrymore acting family came from Philadelphia, as did the celebrated comedian W. C. Fields.

One of the finest singers of the twentieth century was Marian Anderson, who performed both European classical and American traditional music. Other performers and recording artists connected with Pennsylvania include Patti LaBelle, Teddy Pendergrass, Trent Reznor, Christina Aguilera, and Taylor Swift. Born and raised in the Philadelphia area, Will Smith has made a name for himself as the star of films such as *Independence Day*, *Men in Black*, *Ali*, and *Hitch*.

Actor John Barrymore was born in Philadelphia. He is the grandfather of actress Drew Barrymore.

Men in Black, starring Will Smith and Tommy Lee Jones, received three Academy Award nominations in 1997.

Andre Blake played goalkeeper for the Philadelphia Union in their 2015 Lamar Hunt U.S. Open Cup Final match against Sporting Kansas City.

Sports and Recreation

Sports fans in Pennsylvania have much to enjoy. Professional basketball, soccer, hockey, football, and baseball are all played in the state. The Philadelphia 76ers play in the National Basketball Association, and the Philadelphia Union compete in Major League Soccer. The National Hockey League boasts the Philadelphia Flyers and the Pittsburgh Penguins. In football, Philadelphia has the Eagles and Pittsburgh has the Steelers. Major League Baseball fields the Philadelphia Phillies and the Pittsburgh Pirates. Having more than one team per league in several pro sports makes for exciting cross-state rivalries.

The Pittsburgh Steelers are the winningest team in the National Football League, with a record **6 Super Bowl titles**.

Pennsylvania has one of the most extensive **state park systems** in the nation, with more than 100 parks and 3,300 square miles of forest.

Sporting events in Pennsylvania appeal to all age groups. Little League Baseball was founded in Williamsport in 1939 with only three teams. Today, there are thousands of Little League teams around the world. Universities and colleges throughout the state field sports teams for men and women. Almost every collegiate sport is played in the state.

Outdoor sports facilities are abundant. Among the most popular sporting activities in Pennsylvania are fishing, swimming, hiking, and golf. The Pocono Mountains and the Delaware Water Gap are two popular spots. Winter brings snow to the mountain regions, offering opportunities for skiing, snowshoeing, and sledding.

Every year, Williamsport hosts the Little League World Series, which welcomes the best Little League teams from around the world.

There are more than 1.1 million anglers, or people who fish, in Pennsylvania, according to a 2011 survey. On average, Pennsylvanian anglers fish nine days out of the year.

Get To Know
PENNSYLVANIA

Hershey Foods and **H.J. Heinz** are the two biggest food production companies in Pennsylvania. **Hershey** is best known for its **chocolate**, and **Heinz** for its ketchup.

In about 1750, the Conestoga wagon was developed in Lancaster County. Able to carry up to six tons of passengers and cargo, it became a staple of pioneers moving westward during the nineteenth century.

Founded by **Benjamin Franklin**, the **University of Pennsylvania** is one of the nation's oldest schools and is one of the eight prestigious Ivy League colleges in the United States.

EARLY SETTLERS IN PENNSYLVANIA USED THE **GREAT DANE** TO HUNT AND FOR PROTECTION. TODAY, THE GREAT DANE IS THE STATE DOG.

In **1775**, in Philadelphia, Johann Behrent built the **first piano** to be made in the United States. He named it the Piano Forte.

Made in the 1750s, the **Liberty Bell** is made almost entirely of copper and weighs **2,080** pounds.

PITTSBURGH HAS MORE THAN **300 SETS** OF PUBLIC **STAIRS**. IF THEY WERE STACKED ON TOP OF EACH OTHER, THEY WOULD BE MORE THAN 26,000 FEET HIGH.

Brain Teasers

What have you learned about Pennsylvania after reading this book? Test your knowledge by answering these questions. All of the information can be found in the text you just read. The answers are provided below for easy reference.

1 What is the capital of Pennsylvania?

2 What does the name Pennsylvania mean?

3 Where did General Washington and his Continental Army spend the harsh winter of 1777?

4 What is Pennsylvania's highest point?

5 How much of the state is forested?

6 Which Native American groups were living in Pennsylvania when European settlers first arrived?

7 What percentage of population do African Americans account for in the state?

8 Which Pennsylvanian founded the nation's first fire department, hospital, and public lending library?

Key Words

charter: a legal document, often issued by the head of a state or country, granting certain rights and privileges to someone else

dialect: any special variety of a language

estuary: the part of a river where it meets the sea and where fresh and salt water mix

famine: widespread hunger

hydroelectric power: electricity produced by using the force of moving water

metropolitan area: a large city and its surrounding suburbs

modesty: not showing off oneself or one's talents

persecuted: attacked for one's beliefs

reforestation: replanting trees to replace those cut down

rural: relating to the countryside, as opposed to the city

urban: relating to the city, as opposed to the countryside

Index

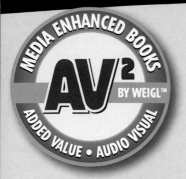

Log on to www.av2books.com

AV² by Weigl brings you media enhanced books that support active learning. Go to www.av2books.com, and enter the special code found on page 2 of this book. You will gain access to enriched and enhanced content that supplements and complements this book. Content includes video, audio, weblinks, quizzes, a slide show, and activities.

AV² Online Navigation

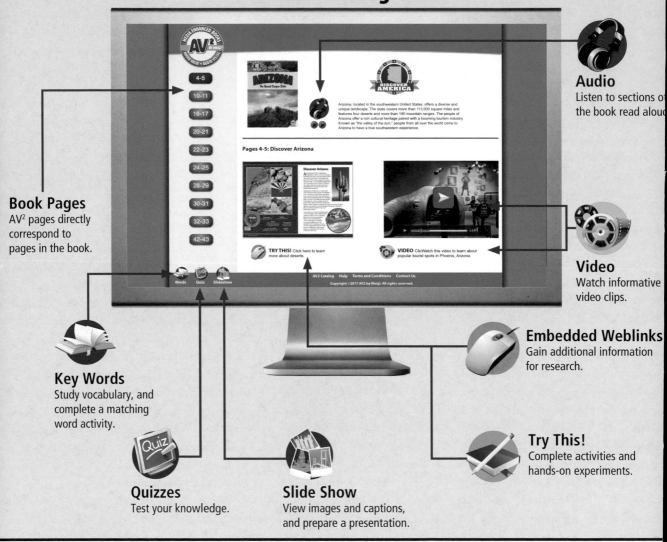

Audio
Listen to sections of the book read aloud

Book Pages
AV² pages directly correspond to pages in the book.

Video
Watch informative video clips.

Key Words
Study vocabulary, and complete a matching word activity.

Embedded Weblinks
Gain additional information for research.

Try This!
Complete activities and hands-on experiments.

Quizzes
Test your knowledge.

Slide Show
View images and captions, and prepare a presentation.

AV² was built to bridge the gap between print and digital. We encourage you to tell us what you like and what you want to see in the future.

Sign up to be an AV² Ambassador at www.av2books.com/ambassador.